T0167269

D A Y L I G H T

A NEW BEGINNING

POEMS

TO PONDER

On
THE ROAD *TO* LIFE

Presented by
Bruce K. Avenell

iUniverse LLC
Bloomington

Poems To Ponder on The Road _TO_ Life

iUniverse books may be ordered through booksellers or by contacting:

iUniverse LLC
1663 Liberty Drive
Bloomington, IN 47403
www.iuniverse.com
1-800-Authors (1-800-288-4677)

ISBN: 978-1-4917-2024-0 (sc)
ISBN: 978-1-4917-2026-4 (e)

Library of Congress Control Number: 2014900201

Printed in the United States of America.

iUniverse rev. date: 03/28/2014

Foreword

Have you ever thought
　Or wondered why,
As life goes speeding,
　Zooming, zooming by,
Why it is … that secret lore,
　The Dragons never, never tell,
Is known to the Unicorn,
　So very, very well?

As a child, I realized I was lost somewhere in a realm that was only an illusion of reality. I was only eight years old, but I already knew there was more to life than this world claimed to offer. As I looked for a way back to reality, I found many things that were clues and finally the way itself. For many beings, this illusion of reality is the only life they know. Creation ever sings its song of life to every living thing. But, if one doesn't listen, then there is no way to hear. The ringing tone you can hear is uniquely yours. The Song of Life is ever there to light your life and fill your days.

Everything in the physical and spiritual universe is alive. Life is the only building block creation has to work with. This planet we live on is alive. While there is a sort of reality to planet earth, we live in the dream of life Father Earth dreams for us. The star we live by is alive. While it has its own reality, Father Earth lives in a dream the star dreams. Our star is part of a galaxy of stars. The galaxy is alive and dreams many, many dreams of life. Our galaxy belongs to a super star, some of which are Silver Stars. Our super star is not a Silver Star. Silver Stars hold many galaxies in their dreams.

Through all the dreams and apparent realities there is a way: A path when you find it; A road when you start to explore it; And a highway when you learn to travel upon it. It is a labyrinth of progressions, which teach you how to manage the energy of divine life. For you are meant to be a divine being in your own right. You must learn how to hold the velocity, energy, and magic of that level of life in your own being.

My poetry is about some of my experiences, observations, and conclusions as I journeyed back along The Road *TO* Life.... Please enjoy... and always remember –

THERE *IS* A WAY

Contents

Far ... Far ... Away

Far beyond the temporal mold,

A rare communion I do hold

That scatters all my earthly fears.

... LOST ...

In the music of the spheres.

??? ... lost ... ???

If you wish to find

Your own true self

!!! ... listen ... !!!

Within the music of the spheres,

And in the secret parts of why,

There *is* a Way.

!!! ... listen ... !!!

The Vital Essence

I asked my Lord for eagles' wings
To ply the burning blue.
"You are a bird," The Great Light said,
"Fly home my love, please do."

I asked the Lord to take my hand
And lead me to his side.
"My song is ever in thy ear.
No hand can reach inside."

I asked the Lord my soul to keep
As dark clouds threatened near.
"The song I sing will keep you safe.
Just listen and you'll hear."

I asked the Lord to think of me
When I am far away.
"There is no near or far at all,"
Was all that He would say.

I asked the Lord that I might live
Contented, free from strife.
"You cannot die my child," He said.
"I've yet to give thee life."

I asked the Lord to bring the light
That drives away all fear.
"You are my unborn child," He said,
"To me, so very dear."

I asked the Lord that I might sit,
Forever by his side.
"You and I were ever one.
From thee I cannot hide."

I asked the Lord to move the clouds
That hide the Silver Sky.
"You made the clouds," He smiled and said.
"Remove them from your eye."

I asked my Lord for eagles wings

To fly into the sun.

"Come home my love, come home," He said.

And now the deed is done.

I asked my Lord to tell me where

The universe had gone?

"While you are free from it," He said,

"The womb goes on and on."

!!! Daylight !!!

On the Road **_TO_** Life.

The paling sky calls me from sleep.
My being thrills in the growing lights.
As day proclaims its mastery of night,
Another day in which to be alive.

Driving darkness relentlessly before it,
Precious daylight marches on.
Commanding fully half the globe,
The morning sun is rising.

But, when this and that and all,
And all, are fully written down,
Our light of life is only just a star.
There are a lot of those around.

Then, when darkness comes,
And claims again the sky,
The stars whisper in their sight,
"There are other ways, other days."

Other precious ways to be alive
In the fragile daylight of a star.
To be awake and conscious,
Involves both near and far.

Other stars conceive other days,
Other precious ways to be alive.
The universe knows many days
And dreams in many nights.

From out amongst the distant stars
Where night seems all prevailing,
Another darkness wanes to brilliant dawn,
The Silver Stars are rising.

Blind and Asleep

On The Road _to_ Life

Plato wrote all men are blind.
As I read his words
I laughed with glee,
For he wrote them down
For all to see.

As my days and years passed,
His words haunted me.
What was that world like
Where all men are blind,
The world that Plato could see?

The morning sun calls awake,
Awake into yet another day.
Is there a light beyond this star,
A day beyond this veil of days,
The world Plato could see?

The ringing sound calls awake,

Awake into a higher, finer day.

Asleep in their dream, few listen

To the song that would set them free.

Lost and alone on The Road _to_ life.

The first step

On The Road _to_ Life

Is to learn how to be awake

Beyond the dream.

!!! Listen. !!!

Waking Up

Asleep in a dream,

I dreamt I could not awake

Until I understood

How it was done.

Awake from the dream,

And fearful of forgetting again,

I carefully reviewed

The awakening process.

And then to my great surprise,

I awoke, yet again,

Into a much more splendid day.

Waking Up Again

Caught in a dream,

I had to force

My way back

To waking consciousness.

Carefully reviewing how

I had brought myself awake,

I awoke, yet again,

Into a brighter day.

That could only happen once,

Once in a lifetime I thought.

But I tried it once again,

And then again and again.

Each time I awoke,

As though from a dream,

To a brighter sweeter day,

More real and alive than before.

Don't dream the dreams
The vendors sell.
Dare to dream the dreams
Your song would tell.

It knows the way _to_ life,
So very, very well.

Within the Dream of Life

The momentums of my life,

Pushed and pulled,

Opposed then accelerated,

Pushed left then right,

Some days up,

Some days down,

Some days there was nothing,

Nothing there at all.

I thought of giving up.

There seemed to be no sense,

No rhyme or reason,

To live a life at all.

In my search for a way to live,

I read of a man

Who dreamt he was a butterfly.

Upon waking he wondered,

Was he a man who dreamt

He was a butterfly

Or was he a butterfly

Dreaming he was a man?

From this I realized
I was living within a dream,
Not a very good dream at that,
But one of my own making.

There are many dreams of life to dream
And many dreams of life to follow.
But they only work,
They only go someplace,
When you learn to dream
Your own dreams of life
According to Creation's rules.
Finding wisdom one soon learns
Creation's laws define reality.
All else is just a wandering dream.

The First Lesson

The first lesson you must learn

On The Road **_TO_** Life

Is how to be awake.

The most important lesson you can learn

On The Road **_to_** Life

Is how to be awake.

Learn how to be awake in this day

And you can learn how to be awake

In the brighter DAYLIGHT of reality.

As all creation knows,

The SILVER STARS are rising.

THERE **IS** A WAY

!!! Listen !!!

Dreams of Morning

I only dreamed to stand in ranks,
A soldier in His corps.
He came and touched my mind with light
And said, "You can be more."

I only dreamed to speak His song,
A note and nothing more.
He came and touched my spine with light
And said, "You can be more."

I only dreamed to stand up straight,
A singer of His song.
He came and touched my spirit with light
And said, "You can be more."

I only dreamed to be a light,
A beacon on His path.
He came and touched my soul with light
And said, "You can be more."

I only dreamed to face the night,
As a light in the gathering dawn.
He came and touched my being with light
And said, "You can be more."

You too can hear the Inner Song,
The ringing in your ear.
Know then, He has touched your life with light
And know – you can be more.

Truth

In the enchanting music of truth,

In the ringing songs of life,

There is a way to know God,

As the stars know God.

Higher up and farther in,

To the music of the spheres,

There is a way to know Deity,

As the galaxies know the Divine.

Still the divine music builds

And higher still there is a way

To know the Creator in the way,

The Silver Stars know their Maker.

The music still lifts you up

As you find within you the way,

To know the Master Creator,

As the universes know,

Their maker and themselves,

On The Road **_TO_** life.

Still on The Road **_TO_** Life,

In those realms beyond

The universes' high domain,
There is a way to know
Who YOU really are.
And that, ... in truth,
Is the real beginning.

Beyond

Beyond the dreams

This life offers,

Another darkness wanes to dawn.

Beyond the dreams

This life has offered,

Another day comes marching.

Beyond the dreams

You were told to dream,

The SILVER STARS are rising.

Beyond your dreams

SEIZE this day.

The SILVER STARS are rising.

Beyond your dreams

SEIZE this day,

This day in the newest dawn.

All creation knows

The SILVER STARS are rising.

Colorado Morning

The morning sun touched the mountain tops,

Bright against a cloudy sky.

In the beauty of that moment,

I saw the clouds as mountains in the sky.

The beauty of that moment, mountains in the sky

Thrilled my imagination.

As I watched the mountains in the sky,

I saw there were Dragons passing by.

Sunlit mountains standing in the sky

With dragons swiftly passing by.

Oh how I wished that I could fly

With the Dragons in the sky.

Called from where I wonder why,

Going perhaps, beyond the sky?

Mountains standing in the sunlit sky

With Dragons swiftly passing by.

All my wisdom I would gladly pay,

To be that way someday,

With the Dragons passing by,

Against the mountains in the sky.

Mountains in the sky,

Dragons passing by,

And I.

The Magic Woods

Alone and lonely I wandered

In a quiet woods

Looking for a path to follow.

Someplace, it seemed far off,

I thought I could hear

Someone sadly crying.

With no path to follow,

I walked toward the sound

Of someone crying.

I was so lonely.

I was near to crying too.

In a quiet glade,

I found a Dragon sobbing.

"Dragon, why are you crying so?"

He looked at me

Through tear filled eyes.

"In all this empty world,

I have no friend at all,"

He said.

"Oh Dragon, I would be so happy

To be your friend."

His joy exploded,

Almost upsetting me.

"Really?"

"Yes, I would really, really,

Love to be your friend."

His joy flooded my heart

With love until it almost burst.

The quiet woods was suddenly alive

With butterflies, and honeybees,

And bunny rabbits too.

We danced about the glade

As new found friends are apt to do,

The Dragon and I,

And the bunny rabbits too.

Exhausted from the joy of dancing,

I lay on the cool sweet grass.

The Dragon lay down beside me.

"Why do you wander in these woods?"

He asked, still breathing hard

From dancing so.

"I'm looking for a path to follow,
A path that goes somewhere."
"There is a path to follow
From here," the Dragon said.
"Where does it start?"
Looking about, I could find no way.
"Right there at your feet,"
Said my new found friend.
Sure enough, at my feet,
I could see a faint trail
Leading off toward
An opening in the trees.
As I followed the faint trail,
It became ever easier to see.
The trail became a track.
The track became a path.
The path became a road.
My Dragon following with me,
"What road are we on?"
I wondered out loud.

Presently, we come to a sign

With an arrow pointing

Along the way

We were going.

In bold letters the sign said,

"The Road _**TO**_ Life."

"But I thought I was alive,"

I said somewhat taken aback.

"There is much more to life,

Than one can imagine here,"

The Dragon said as we moved on.

A while later I thought,

"I wonder where this road goes."

Again a little farther on,

There was a sign beside the road.

An arrow pointed to the direction

We were going.

"To love, laughter, magic, joy,

And the great happiness,"

The sign read.

Presently, we came to a rise

And could see far ahead.

The road stretched off

To the far horizon.

There far off before us

The sky glowed in silver light

As though, another day was coming.

"It's a very long way to go,"

I said surveying the distance.

A flock of birds flew by

Seeming to follow the road.

"I wish I could fly," I said.

"I can fly," the Dragon offered,

"Climb on my back."

And we flew off

Following the birds.

Flying above the road

There was much more to see.

In the far distance

A new day was coming.

A Silver Star was rising,

To a new morning, ... on,

The Road to Life.

In joy we flew

Towards the new dawn

And the great happiness,

My Dragon and I

on

The Road **_TO_** Life.

The Dragon on the Road

Along the path I took that day,

A Dragon lay

And blocked my way.

Unafraid I faced him,

Eye to blazing eye.

Thus impressed he told me

All the secret parts of ***why***,

Of you and me,

And why we be,

As life goes speeding, SPEEDING by.

In the magic

Of that moment,

As I faced him

Eye to blazing eye,

He told me

In the secret parts of why,

"If there is no magic,

No joy in your life,

Then there is no Dragon

In your life."

Across the adventures of my years,

I've learned to tell,

It is only my Dragon,

Who knows me well.

In the Secret Parts of Why

Another path,

Another day,

And again I found

The Dragon blocked my way.

"You told me,

All the secret parts of why.

What more is there to know?

Why do you block my path today?"

Quietly the Dragon offered,

"Have you not noticed,

The path you take

Is more the same,

The further on you go?"

"But it is my path

I chose to take.

Why do you block it so?"

He beckoned me to come close

And then closer still.

Then very quietly he said,

"There is a Road **_TO_** Life,

Which leads one beyond

This vague dream of life."

"Oh Dragon I have searched

And searched for the Road _**TO**_ Life.

But even in the secret

Parts of why,

There is no reason why

I have not found it."

Again he beckoned me close,

And then again closer still.

Quietly as though to keep

The secret of it he said,

"Even now you're standing in the middle

Of The Road _to_ Life."

I looked about and could see

No sign at all of any road.

"Some say," the Dragon offered,

"The Road is broader than it is long.

But the truly wise know

The Road _to_ Life is much longer

Than it is wide."

"How can I follow a road
When I cannot even find
The width of it?" said I
Wondering how I could ever
Find my way.
"Climb on my back,"
He offered, "the road
Is much easier to follow
When you can fly."

Paths

There are many paths,

Which promise to be

The true path home.

But why bother wandering about?

Even in the secret parts of why,

THERE _**IS**_ A WAY.

!!! . . . LISTEN . . . !!!

Legend

Have you ever thought
   Or wondered why,
As life goes speeding,
   Zooming, zooming by,
Why it is … that secret lore,
   The Dragons never, never tell,
Is known to the Unicorn,
   So very, very well?

And why … that special secret magic,
   That Wizards use and know,
Of why we come and live and love,
   And where there is to go,
That masters Dragons in the sky,
   Commanding … eye to blazing eye,
That holds the secret mystic key,
   Of fate and fame and eternity,
That is privileged to that secret lore,
   The Dragons never, never tell,
Is known to the Unicorn,
   So very, very well?

And why … all the wisdom,

    That was ever born,

Cannot buy the friendship

    Of the Unicorn?

Though it command that secret lore,

    The Dragons never, never tell,

It does not impress the Unicorn,

    So very, very well.

Well … Unicorns and Dragons too,

    Know all the parts of why,

Of you and me, and why we be,

    As life goes … speeding, speeding by.

But … while Dragons wing from sun to sun,

    And might someday tell you why,

None can match the Unicorn,

    In knowing … … … where to fly.

A Basket of Roses

All seven Lords covet the Silver Rose.

Not one can say its bearer "No,"

Nor raise his sword against the bloom,

The Silver Warriors grow.

  Rose and eagle on my shield,

  That shines as with the sun.

  Come sing a little song with me,

  And I will give thee one.

All seven Lords covet this special rose.

Oh, yes, they have roses too.

But none can hold the Silver Rose,

The warriors grow for you.

  Rose and eagle on my shield,

  That shines as with the sun.

  Come sing a little song with me,

  And I will give thee one.

All seven Lords bow to the Silver Rose,

As they are bound to do.

For he who planted Silver Roses,

Also planted them … and you.

> Rose and eagle on my shield,
>
> That shines as with the sun.
>
> Come sing a little song with me,
>
> And I will give thee one.

All seven lords covet the Silver Rose.

For they are sure to know,

That far beyond the Silver Sun,

The Silver Warriors go.

> Rose and eagle on my shield,
>
> That shines as with the sun.
>
> Come sing a little song with me
>
> That I might give thee one.

Ascension

We stood on a silver beach.

To the west, in early morning,

A silver sea broke on the silver sand.

To the east, announcing the dawn,

A Silver Sun, still low, in the silver sky.

Seven white unicorns stood before us,

With silver hooves and silver horns.

Five held mounted warriors.

"Are we going to follow them?"

She asked, in wonder of this place,

Not having been this way before.

"It wouldn't be proper,"

I said, helping her to mount.

"Why Not?" She was surprised.

"Because I'm their leader,"

I said as I mounted my steed.

And we road off,

Into the Silver Star.

Yesterdays' Tomorrows

My eyes are young.

My sight is old.

My vision well remembers yesterday.

Not yesterday to this and that,

But yesterday when the pyramids of Giza

Were still a fantastic dream.

My eyes are young.

My sight is old.

My vision still dreams of yesterday.

Not yesterday to this and that,

But yesterday when Stonehenge

Was still a fantastic dream.

My eyes are young.

My sight is old.

My vision still remembers yesterday.

Not yesterday to this and that,

But yesterday when Teotihuacan

Was still a fantastic dream.

My eyes are young.
My sight is old.
My vision still dreams of yesterdays.
Not yesterdays to this and that,
But yesterday when the Parthenon
Was still a fantastic dream.

My eyes are young.
My soul is old.
My being still dreams of tomorrow.
Not tomorrow to this and that,
But tomorrow when Daylight comes.
For all creation knows
The Silver Stars are rising.

Keeping Up With Time

Time moves on.
It passes us by.
But in only a moment,
It comes again and
Passes us by again.

Time moves on,
As we stand still.
But how does one stand still
In a universe where
Everything is moving?

Time moves on,
Nor answers any
Of our questions,
Of who we are,
Of where we're going.

Time moves on,

And on, and on,

Pursuing its tomorrows.

Where have we been?

Where are we going?

Time only knows.

There _is_ a way.

The Chimes of Time

The songs of life

Are clearer now.

The notes

Much easier to hear

As though a bell chimes

Constantly deep

Within your ear.

As though a bell chimes

Constantly from far

And away in time,

Now, oh wanderer,

Find your pathway home.

Time's hour is late

And you must return

Before the last notes

Chime.

Before the last notes

Chime

Far and away in time.

The Kannon

It is only a moment,
As any other moment.
As all the other moments,
It is only just a moment.

Spin your aura in,
In this so common moment.
Focus on being here, now,
In this expectant moment.

Let go of all the dreams
You have longed to dream.
Let go of all the Wisdom
You have longed to hold.

Be still in the great silence.
Be still in the great starlight.
Be still in your racing heart
As you step beyond the day.

Be still within your stillness.
Be still at the speed of light.
Find the velocity of life,
Awake in a moment, and alive.

Remember

Drink of the water of life

As often as you can.

For whatsoever

Commands your attention

More than it,

Shall rule your days.

Duja

About the Game

Life is only just a game.

Play the game of life.

Enjoy the game of life.

Eat and drink,

Laugh and dance,

Sing and be merry.

But know you this, my friend,

It is only the wizards here

Who are real,

And will live beyond

This moment's fling.

For all else,

Life has yet to begin.

Wizard school begins

Before the crack of dawn.

!!! *Listen* !!!

THERE _IS_ A WAY

The Mystery

The ages come and the ages go
Then incarnate once again.
Man stripped of his old disguise
Must build his stage again.

The ages come, forget their past
And build on newer dreams.
Man stripped of all his yesterdays
Hardly dares to dream new dreams.

The ages live among the stars,
Who hold so many dreams.
Man lost in all his yesterdays
Hardly dares to dream it seems.

The ages swing amongst the stars
And have the universe to roam.
Man lost in his dreamless day
Must find his own way home.

Each age tells a path.
Each age holds a clue.
Each age has forgotten.
The way is up to you.

It is time love.
It is time now
To come home –

Listen.

There *is* a Way...

To know what the stars know,

To know what the galaxies know,

To know what the super stars know,

To know what the silver stars know,

To know what the universe knows,

To know what the universes know,

To graduate from this school of life,

And reach the end of time,

And a new beginning

On

THE ROAD *TO* LIFE.

!!! . . . listen . . . !!!

Going Nowhere

Believe nothing

Of what I tell you

But this,

It is your beliefs

That hold you a prisoner

In these lower realms' dreams of life.

In these realms of

Time, Illusion and Paradox,

Look beyond these illusions

In these dreams of life

And you may find

The Road _**TO**_ Life.

Always, always remember

There _**IS**_ a Way.

Victory

I asked Deity, "Where did you come from?"

And He said to me,

"I come from sweetness and light,

Laughter and joy,

Magic and merriment,

Plenty and multitudes,

Eternal realms of life.

I am as you are.

I grow as you grow.

I come and I go

And my song is eternal.

My song is eternal,

As I come and go.

I am nowhere.

I am everywhere.

And the paradox is the key

To life and to me.

We are one.

Yet, you are one.

GOD if you dare.

LORD if you share.

<u>DIVINE</u> if *YOU* find the way."

Then he showed me a sword,
Held vertically in alignment,
And He said,

"Victory."

Horizons

My mother's horizons
Were too small for me.
My father's horizons
Stretched from sea to sea.
As a child my horizons
Were all my eyes could see.

I was lost in a world of illusion,
Until the night sky talked to me,
For all I have learned of this and that,
Of what men are and aspire to be.
It was the night sky that spoke to me
And the music of the stars
That set me free.

The song of life
Was quite enough to hold.
It was only for very special souls,
Not for every man, I was told.
While I felt I was no more,
Just a man, no more than any other,
The stars in the sky said, "Come higher.
There is much more to know, brother."

The song of songs,

The music of the stars,

Is truly the royal nectar of life.

But is in all its sweetness,

Only just the nectar of life.

One must learn the sheer joy

Of dancing with the Silver Stars

To find the true path home,

Beyond the far horizons,

On The Road **_TO_** Life.

The Piper

As I stood watching,

A piper came a walking,

Playing on a silver flute,

A brilliant silver flute,

A clear and haunting melody,

With notes of blue and silver,

Spinning off into the ether,

Spinning and gaining strength,

In their harmonies and melodies,

Gaining and growing,

Spinning and dancing,

Harmonies and melodies,

And haunting silver music.

Each note blue and silver,

Playing about the piper,

Grew stronger and sweeter,

Spinning and dancing,

Lighter and brighter,

And stronger and sweeter,

And as real as the piper.

And they walked with him,
Living silver music,
And to each in their time,
To each walking in time,
He gave a silver flute,
A brilliant silver flute.
And they followed with Him,
And they played with him,
A little way with him,
Until they caught the music's
Haunting, silver melodies.
Then each walked their own way
And the harmonies and melodies,
Grew stronger and sweeter,
Blue and silver music,
Spinning and dancing,
Higher and sweeter,
And stronger and stronger.
And I was caught up in it,
A great crescendo of music,

Haunting silver music,
Spinning and dancing,
And I was real,
Spinning and dancing,
Laughing and dancing,
Laughing and flying,
Laughing, dancing, flying,
And as real as the piper!

Oh, listen carefully,
Children of the silence,
One breathless moment.
IT IS THE TIME
OF THE PIPER!

!!! Listen !!!

!!! . . . LISTEN . . . !!!

There is a way to learn,
What the stars have learned.

!!! . . . LISTEN . . . !!!

There is a way to know
What the stars have dreamed.

!!! . . . LISTEN . . . !!!

There is a way to know
What the stars will tell you.

!!! . . . LISTEN . . . !!!

There is much more to know,
That the stars **_can_** tell you.

!!! . . . LISTEN . . . !!!

There is much more to know,
Than the stars _will_ tell you.

!!! . . . LISTEN . . . !!!

There is much more to know,
Than the stars _can_ tell you.

!!! . . . LISTEN . . . !!!

On The Road _TO_ Life

!!! … Listen … !!!

The Next Eternity

You can know what the stars know.
You can speak to them all,
If you enter the night slightly,
And softly do protocol.

You can know what the stars know.
You can see what they see,
If you enter the night lightly,
And tell them you're free.

You can know what the stars know.
You can dream with their dreams,
If you enter the night rightly,
It can be, as it seems.

You can know what the stars know
As they stand across time,
If you find the right focus,
And are free of your mind.

You can know what the stars know.
They will show you the way.
If you dream in their dreams,
You can hear what they say.

You can know what the stars know.
It is so destined to be.
If you find the nights song,
And sing it to thee.

You can know what the galaxies know
As those risen on high,
If you're free of your mind
And have learned how to fly.

You can know what the galaxies know
As they dance in their time.
Just hold the night's song
And thrice make it rhyme.

Just hold the night's song
And thrice . . . make it rhyme.

Are You Coming?

Seek thou the Song

Our Father Sings.

He sings His Song to me

And the night is over.

Sing thou the Song

Our Father Sings.

I Sing his Song to thee

And we are free.

!!! … listen … !!!

!!! … Remember … !!!

ALL THE WIT OF WIZARDRY

HAS REACHED ITS RIGHTFUL END

WHEN, AT LAST YOU HAVE,

A DRAGON FOR A FRIEND.

THERE IS A WAY

on

THE ROAD *TO* LIFE

!!! . . . LISTEN . . . !!!

Long Memory

Each individual being has three mind structures that include memory. The *temporal mind* includes the current life memories. The *spirit mind*, or super conscious mind, I have followed back a bit beyond the limits of my interest, which is why I came to incarnate in Lemuria. The third mind is the memory of one's eternal being. When one is truly immortal and living in the realm I call the Great Happiness beyond this universe of universes, all memory is available. But it seems only the eternal moment matters. I have had significant roles in history on several occasions and learned that it is much more fun being "nobody" than it is being "somebody." The poetry I share with you is about moments that were important to me. You must be center stage in your own life to find The Road *TO* Life, … Listen … Children of the silence, one breathless moment, it is the time of the piper. On The Road *TO* Life, when you have learned again how to hear, YOU can learn what the stars have to teach you. And that is a real beginning.

For more information, please contact us:

The Eureka Society
P.O. Box 3117
Montrose, Colorado 81402

Or

970-417-4822